New Kindle Fire HD Manual (Kindle Fire HD 8 and 10)

The complete user guide with instructions from basic start up to advance user (December 2017)

Corey Stone

including specific information will be considered an illegal act irrespective of if it is done electronically or in print. This extends to creating a secondary or tertiary copy of the work or a recorded copy and is only allowed with express written consent from the Publisher. All additional rights reserved.

The information in the following pages is broadly considered to be a truthful and accurate account of facts and as such any inattention, use or misuse of the information in question by the reader will render any resulting actions solely under their purview. There are no scenarios in which the publisher or the original author of this work can be in any fashion deemed liable for any hardship or damages that may befall them after undertaking information described herein.

Additionally, the information in the following pages is intended only for informational purposes and should thus be thought of as universal. As befitting its nature, it is presented without assurance regarding its prolonged validity or interim quality. Trademarks that are mentioned are done without written consent and can in no way be considered an endorsement from the trademark holder.

TABLE OF CONTENTS

Introduction

Thank you and congratulations for purchasing *"New Kindle Fire HD Manual (Kindle Fire HD 8 and 10): The complete user guide with instructions from basic start up to advance user (December 2017)"*.

This complete user guide will walk you through the step-by-step process of using your Kindle Fire HD. Everything you need to know in order to easily operate your device from the moment you take it out of the box is included in this extensive guide, ensuring that you can get the most from your Kindle Fire HD. This book is also perfect for anyone who may be wanting to customize their experience with their tablet or who may be discovering issues with their device. This book can help you to troubleshoot your device and overcome common problems that many device users face so that you can continue to enjoy your Kindle Fire HD experience.

This eBook is excellent for being downloaded onto your Kindle device directly so that you can easily access it anytime you need help with using your device. If you are ready to begin getting the most out of your Kindle Fire HD tablet right away, then please read on!

Chapter 1: Getting Started with Your Fire HD

If you are new to your device, you may be wondering about how you can use certain functions on it. This chapter will help you discover what features you should know how to use on your Kindle Fire HD tablet. From starting the device to completely charging it, and where to find important information such as your settings. You will learn all of the basics that you need to know about your device right here in Chapter 1!

Starting the Device

Starting your Kindle Fire HD is very simple. On the bottom right section of your Fire HD, you will discover a power button. Simply press and hold this button for 2-3 seconds and your device will begin turning on. If you find that you need to restart your device, or you want to turn it off, simply hold this button once again. A screen will come up, prompting you to turn off the device. You can select "OK" if you choose to turn it off, then simply turn it back on again to restart it.

Battery and Controls

With your screen turned on, you will notice the top of the screen features a status bar that provides you with a variety of important information about your Kindle Fire HD device. Here, you will be able to see your battery indicator. This will let you know how much charge is remaining on your device. You can also find any notifications that you may have from applications you use such as games, e-mails, or the music player. You can quickly tap the display setting to use commonly performed tasks, such as adjusting the volume on your device, locking or unlocking the screen rotation, adjusting display brightness levels, and more. If you need more settings than those shown on the status bar, simply tap the plus sign beneath it that says "more" to reveal additional settings options. The final piece of information you will find in the status bar is your Wi-Fi information. Here, you can view the status of your Wi-Fi, and learn about the strength of your connection. You may also see different Wi-Fi indicators if you are not connected, or if you are connected to an internet hotspot.

First Time Charging

To charge your Kindle Fire, you will need to use the charging cable provided when you purchased the device. Simply plug it into the port located on the bottom of the device, between the headphone jack and the power button.

IMPORTANT NOTE: *Allow the device to completely drain before charging it for the first time, and allow it to completely charge before using it again.*

The charging indicator light on your Kindle Fire HD device will light up orange when it is charging, and green when the charge is completed. You should note that completely charging a device can take up to four hours, so your first charge may take quite some time, especially if you allow the device to completely discharge first.

Registering Your Fire

In order to access all of the features that have been made available on your device, you need to register it with Amazon. You can do this by simply registering the device to your unique Amazon account. You will have to ensure that your device is connected to Wi-Fi before you can register it, so do this first. Then, you can tap the quick settings icon and click the "more" button to access your complete list of settings.

7

From there, you will find an option that shows "My Account". Upon clicking this button, you will be walked through the step-by-step process to register your device so that you can access all of the Kindle Fire HD features and get the most out of your device.

Storage and The Cloud Drive

Although your Kindle Fire HD has built-in storage, you can also link it to your Cloud account to ensure that your device remains backed up. The Cloud service is free to Kindle HD users, and provides you with additional space to store your content. In order to access content from the cloud, simply tap what you want and begin using it *without* downloading it. If you want access to it later, such as when you are out of Wi-Fi range, then you can download the content and begin using it.

Learning to Navigate

Navigating your Kindle Fire HD is simple. Beneath the status bar, you will notice a search bar. You can use this to search for anything you may be looking for. Below the search bar, you will discover another navigation bar that features these options:

- Newsstand
- Books
- Music
- Video
- Docs
- Apps
- Web

You can click any of these buttons and browse the available content at your leisure.

On your Kindle Fire HD homepage, there is a carousel that allows you to swipe through any content you have recently been using. Books, movies, music, and other recent activity will show up in this carousel. This will allow you to quickly and effortlessly switch between applications to view additional content.

Below the carousel there is a docking tray where you can pin your favorite applications to. This enables you to access any of your favorite content quickly and effortlessly, as you will not have to scroll through the carousel to find it.

Changing the Wallpaper

To change the wallpaper on your home screen, simply access the settings in your Kindle Fire HD by going to your quick settings option and then tapping the "more" selection. There, you will find a setting called "display". Choose that option, then choose the "wallpaper" option. There, you will see the "change" option that allows you to change the wallpaper to anything you would like.

Bluetooth Pairing

To activate your Bluetooth pairing option with your Kindle Fire HD device, begin by swiping down from the top of the screen. There, you will see the "Quick Settings" menu. Choose the "Bluetooth" option and then tap the switch that appears next to this option. When it turns orange, this means your device is ready to be paired.

Next, go into your "more settings" option and find the "pair a Bluetooth device option". In that setting, you will discover any available pairing devices. Choose the device you want to pair it with and then follow any prompts on the screen to pair the two devices. When they have paired, there will be a Bluetooth indicator with two arrows facing inward toward the Bluetooth icon to show you the pairing has been successful. If the arrows do not exist and there is simply a Bluetooth logo, your pairing has been unsuccessful and you will need to try again.

The Internet and Your Fire HD Device

Wi-Fi

Swipe down from the top of your Kindle Fire HD screen to access the quick settings menu. From there, tap the "wireless" option. Once you have, you will see an option next to the Wi-Fi setting to turn the Wi-Fi "on". Choose the network you want to connect to, and input your network password if there is one. The Wi-Fi will then be connected. If it is not connected, check to ensure that your Airplane Mode is off.

Wi-Fi Airplane Mode

You cannot use Wi-Fi in airplane mode on your Kindle Fire HD 8 or 10. However, you can put your device into Airplane Mode as needed. Note that this setting will turn off your Wi-Fi automatically, however. To do so, access your quick settings menu by swiping down from the top of the screen. Then, tap the "Airplane mode" option. Your Airplane mode will now be activated. To turn it off, simply click the button once more.

Payment

In order to speed up the payment process, your Kindle Fire HD has the option for you to input your payment settings. Upon doing so, you can then simply click "pay" on any checkout screen and the device will automatically use the preset payment option that you have inputted. This is helpful when purchasing eBooks, movies, or music on your device.

To complete this process, access your Amazon account from a computer. Then, access the settings menu and click "edit payment method" beneath the "digital payment settings" headline. From there, you can input your credit card information from any card of your choosing. After entering the credit card information, click continue. The next screen will enable you to input your billing and shipping addresses, where products will automatically be sent to, if a physical product exists in the purchase. When you are done, you can review your settings. Your 1-Click payment method will now be completed and can be used on any device you have that is connected to your Amazon account, including your Kindle Fire HD.

Social Networks

Your tablet has the option for you to connect your device to social networks, such as Facebook or Twitter. There, you can share statuses about what you are reading, notes about said books, and even book ratings and highlights. To do this, you want to access your quick settings menu by swiping down from the top of the home screen. Then, choose the "more" option to access your full settings list. From there, you can choose the "manage social network accounts" option. Choose the desired social network you want to link to your device and enter your login information. When you have, click "done". Your device will now be connected!

Internet Browser

Along the navigation menu on your Kindle Fire HD, you will notice there is an option called "Web". If you want to access an particular internet browser from your device, simply select this option. A browser window will pop up, enabling you to search for anything you desire to look for.

Email

Setting up your email with your Kindle Fire HD is simple. Go into your "apps" section, and once prompted, enter your email address. Then, select "next". Enter the password for your account on the next screen, and then select "next" again. Your email account will then be configured to your device. Once it has been configured, you will click "next" once more. Then, your device will be completely synchronized with your emails. You will now be able to access your email, and get notifications when you receive new emails through your Kindle Fire HD device.

Calendar

Your device is equipped with a useable calendar that can be organized to provide you with any information you require to help you remember upcoming events. To set up your calendar, go to the "app" section and locate your calendar. When you initially open the app, it will be completely blank. Simply tap "new event" to input any new events that you want your device to remind you of. The following screen will provide you with the opportunity to input any desired information regarding the event. Click "done" when you have inputted all of the information. You will be returned to the calendar screen, where you can new view your new event.

Contacts

You can store contact information in your Kindle Fire HD device to make it easier for you to recall important contact information for friends, family, coworkers, or anyone else. Simply go into your "app" section and select the "contacts" option. At first, your list will be blank. However, you can easily choose the "new contact" option and input any contact information you have for your new contact. When you have completed inputting the information, select "done" and your device will store the information. You will now be able to access your new contact from the contact screen.

All About Apps

How to Download Apps and Games

You can download a variety of games on your Kindle Fire HD device. To do so, simply go to the "App" option in your navigation menu.

There, you will see the option to purchase and download new apps. Simply select this option and browse the games and applications that are available on your device. Once you have found one you wish to install, you can easily download it by simply selecting the "download" button. If there are any fees associated with the app, you will be informed of that on the screen prior to choosing the "download" option. By agreeing to download the app, you will be allowing Amazon to charge the credit card on your account, if you have one stored there.

Learning to Uninstall Apps and Games

If you no longer want an application or game on your device, simply go to the quick settings menu on your device by swiping down from the top of the screen. There, you want to click "more" so that you can access the settings for your device. Select the option listed as "manage all applications". Then, swipe right so that you can view all of your applications. Choose the app you no longer want stored in your device, and then select the "uninstall" option. The application or game will now be uninstalled from your Kindle Fire HD.

Chapter 2: Shopping and Entertainment

The Kindle Fire HD tablets are well-known for helping you effortlessly shop and access entertainment! If you want to get the most out of your device, you *must* know how to access these features. Use this chapter to help you with everything related to enjoying shopping and entertainment on your Kindle Fire HD tablet.

Reading On Your Fire

How to Buy and Read Books, Magazines, and Periodicals

Begin by ensuring that you are connected to Wi-Fi, as you cannot download anything without this connection. Then, from the home screen on your Kindle Fire HD 8 or 10 select the "books" option. Once you are there, you will see a button called "store" in the top right corner of the screen, below the battery indicator. Select this option, and your device will take you to the Kindle store. From the store, you can browse through all of the titles that are available on the Kindle Fire HD. When you are ready, select the title you want. Then, you can tap the "buy" button on the right side of the information screen.

To purchase magazines or other reading material, simply chose the respective option in your navigation menu, such as the "Newsstand" option.

How to Transfer Books from Your Old Device

Transferring your old books to your new device is extremely simple on the Kindle Fire HD 8. To do so, start by connecting your old Kindle device to your PC through the USB port. Then, under the "My Computer" section on your PC, open the device's documents. From there, drag any documents you want to keep into a folder on your PC. When you are done, eject the device and remove it from your PC. Then, plug in your new Kindle Fire HD device through the USB port, and open it up in the same way. Select the "My Computer" option and open the device on your PC. Dag and drop the folders that you previously dropped onto your PC into your new Kindle's folders. Wait for them to finish transferring, and then eject the Kindle from the PC and remove the cord. When you turn on your new Kindle device now, it should have all of the books you transferred from your old device in its library.

Reading Basics

Reading books on your new Kindle Fire HD device is simple. Simply go to the "books" section in the navigation menu. From there, you will be able to see all of the titles in your library. Select the one you want to read and click on the name. The book will open up and you will be brought to the reading screen where you can now start reading your book on the device.

How to Purchase and Listen to Audio

Adding Music

Purchasing and listening to music on your Kindle Fire HD is simple. Begin by selecting the "Music" option in your navigation menu from the home screen. Then, you can tap the "store" option. You will then see a prompt come up that requires you to authorize audio listening through your device from your Amazon Music account. You want to authorize it so that you can use your Amazon Music library on your device. When you have, you can use the "search" tool to choose any song you want to listen to. Once you have found it, simply open the song on your app. You will see all of the song's information, including an option to purchase it. Click "buy" or "buy now" and confirm your purchase when you are ready.

How to Listen to Your Music

After purchasing music to listen to on your device, listening to the music itself is incredibly easy. Simply select the "go to library" option from the purchasing screen, or "music" in the navigation bar. You will then be brought to your musical library. From there, pick the song you want to listen to and tap the play button next to its title. You will then be able to listen to the song you have chosen.

How to Listen to Audiobooks

Listening to audiobooks on your Kindle Fire HD is as simple as listening to music on it. Simply return to the home screen on your device and find the "audiobook" option in your navigation menu. Once you have found it, click on that option. From there, you will be taken to your audiobook library. You can select any audiobook in your library and begin listening to it immediately. If you do not currently have an audiobook library, or if you are searching for a new one, you can simply tap the "store" option in the top right section of your screen, below the battery indicator. From there, you can browse through Amazon's selection of audiobooks and purchase any you desire. After purchasing them, they will automatically be downloaded into your audiobook library.

Importing Your Music Library from Other Sources

If you already own the rights to a song but you want to listen to it on your Amazon Kindle device, you can easily import music to your library. Simply ensure the tracks are downloaded on your PC, then plug your Kindle Fire HD device into it using the USB cable. When it is connected, select "My Computer" and locate your Fire HD files on your PC. Then, drag and drop any music files you want into your Kindle Fire HD documents. When you are done, eject the device and remove it from your PC. Then, you can listen to the music through your music library on your Kindle Fire HD.

How to Purchase and Watch Videos

How to Open and Play Videos

Similar to other applications, your Kindle Fire HD has a built-in button for accessing videos on your device. Begin by heading to the home screen. Then, in the navigation bar, you will find a button called "videos". Click this button.

When you're there, tap the "Library" button that is in the top-right section of your screen. You can then tap on the cloud tab, and click any video you wish to view. Anything you have rented or purchased with your Kindle device will be viewable in this folder.

How to Transfer Your Own Videos to Your Fire HD

Instead of purchasing directly on your tablet, you can also transfer files that you already have onto your Kindle Fire HD. Simply plug your device into your computer and open the file that contains all of your Kindle Fire HD documents. Usually, this can be found through "My Computer" on a PC, or simply on the desktop display of your computer on a Mac. Open the documents and navigate to the "video" folder. There, you can drop any video files from your computer onto your device. Once you eject and unplug your device from your computer, you should be able to find these videos in your Kindle Fire HD video library using the same navigation techniques as outlined in the previous tip ("How to Open and Play Videos").

Watch Your Movies on Your TV

If you own an Amazon Fire TV Box or Amazon Fire TV Stick for your television, you can watch videos from your Kindle Fire HD on your television. To do so, simply ensure that both devices (Fire TV and Fire tablet) are connected to the same wireless network, and that your Fire TV device is properly connected to your television. Once you have verified that connection, go into the settings for your Fire TV device and find the "Display & Sounds" section. There, you can turn on "Second Screen Notifications", allowing you to control the television from your Fire tablet. Once you have control, you can navigate to the video or photo on your tablet that you wish to display on your TV, and then use the screen icon (a black rectangle with a white arrow that points upward) on your device to display the video or photograph on your television.

How to Rent Movies or TV Shows

After you have activated the 1-click payment method (See "Payments"), you can easily rent or buy movies and TV shows on your Kindle Fire HD. Simply go to the home page on your tablet and find the "Videos" section in the navigation bar. Then, from there you can tap on the magnifying glass ("search") and search for specific titles. Alternatively, you can swipe to the right, from the left edge of the screen, to begin browsing titles that Amazon has picked. When you have found a title you are interested in, open it by clicking on the title. Then, you can either choose to "rent" or "buy" it on the detail page. There are two definitions you can choose from when you are buying videos, standard or high-definition. Once you confirm your purchase, the purchase will automatically be processed on the payment method you have linked to your 1-click payment option with your Amazon account.

Camera and Documents

How to Transfer Photos to Your Kindle Fire HD

To transfer photos onto your Kindle Fire HD 8 or 10, you simply need to plug the device into your PC. Then, open the files by either opening them directly on the desktop of a Mac, or by going through the "My Computer" folder on a PC. When you do, open the folder that says "photos" and choose which photographs you want to transfer. Simply drag and drop the files from your PC onto your tablet files. If you want to transfer the files from your tablet and onto your computer, drop them in the other direction. That is, drag the files from your tablet documents onto your desktop. When you are done, eject the device before unplugging it from your PC.

Storing Pictures and Personal Videos in the Amazon Cloud Drive

The majority of your purchases will be stored within the Amazon Cloud Drive automatically, but you can also store your personal documents there as well, to prevent yourself from using up valuable space on your tablet. To store personal documents on the Amazon Cloud Drive, simply send the documents to your Amazon Kindle Email Address. To do that, you first need to ensure that the address you are sending from has been approved on your Personal Document Settings.

So, first you want to go to your Amazon browser and into your account. From there, you can select "Manage Your Content and Devices". Find the settings section and choose "Personal Document Settings". You can then add your approved e-mail address and confirm the approval.

Next, you want to set up your "Send to" Kindle Email Address. To do that, you want to go back to your Amazon browser tab to the "Manage Your Content and Device" settings. Then, go into your settings and once again choose "Personal Document Settings". There, you can choose "Send-to-Kindle Email Settings". Under this section you will find your Send-to-Kindle email address. Simply highlight it and add it to your contacts on your Kindle Fire HD so that you can easily send documents to it later.

When you are ready, start an e-mail in your Kindle tablet's email section. Ensure that you are sending it *to* your "send to" Kindle email address, and *from* your approved address. Attach the documents you want to send, up to 25 documents per email. After you click send, the documents will be uploaded into your Amazon Kindle Cloud Drive!

Using the Fire's Built-In Camera App

Many people who use the Kindle Fire HD wonder where the file for using the camera is. The built-in front facing camera is great for using when it comes to making video calls through the Skype application, but accessing the camera just to take pictures is a bit harder. First, you want to go to the application installer. Then, you want to search for and download the "ES File Explorer". This is a free application that will help you access hidden files and applications on your Kindle Fire HD. This is located right in the Amazon App store, so it is easy to download right to your tablet device.

Once you download the application, you want to launch the application and tap the "AppMgr" button located at the top of the screen. Next, you want to select "category". A window will pop up titled "Select Types", and you want to choose "System apps". Then, all of the hidden applications on your Kindle Fire HD tablet will be available for you to view. Among them will be the camera, which you can use to take pictures and videos directly on your device.

Viewing Photos with the Camera Roll

In order to access the photographs that you have taken with your camera, you will need to open the camera application once again. You will launch it using the same strategy you used in the previous tip, "Using the Fire's Built-In Camera App". Then, you will see the most recent photograph you have taken. Click that and your entire camera roll will pop up!

Chapter 3: Troubleshooting and Common Issues

As with many devices, the Kindle Fire HD 8 and 10 tablets have their own set of common issues that users have faced. This section is completely up-to-date with all of the most discussed issues up to this point. If you are experiencing any troubles with your device, you should be able to find the trouble here so that you can rectify the issue quickly! Keep this manual handy so you can access this part of the guide anytime you may face issues with your device.

Cannot Connect to Wi-Fi

If Wi-Fi is not working on your device, there are a few steps you can try to rectify the issue. First, you want to ensure that other devices are connecting to your home network without issue, and that your airplane mode is turned off. You also want to make sure that your device has been updated to the latest software issue. After that, if it is still not working, you want to ensure that you are using the proper password to access the Wi-Fi connection. If you are, the next step is to try turning off the Wi-Fi and then turning it back on. This will restart the Wi-Fi connection so that you can try accessing it once again. Sometimes the Wi-Fi connectivity has a glitch, and restarting it can help you connect to the internet. If this doesn't work, try restarting your Kindle Fire. If you are still struggling to connect to the internet, check your Wi-Fi range and make sure you are close enough to connect. You can also try restarting your router and modem, as this can restart the internet itself and help it connect to devices better.

Battery Not Holding a Charge

Some people purchase their Kindle Fire HD tablets and discover that the battery does not hold a charge very well. It may die quickly, making it feel as though you are constantly charging it just to get a few minutes of use out of it. Take note that this is not normal behavior for your tablet and that it should hold a fairly lengthy charge, allowing you to get adequate use before having to charge it again. There are a few solutions you can try before contacting the manufacturer (Amazon) to have the issue rectified. First, you can try holding the power button down for 20 seconds, to complete a hard shutdown. Then, you can plug it in, letting it charge completely before using it again. If this doesn't work, check the cable that you are using. You should always use the cable that came with your Kindle Fire HD, as this cable was designed to transfer plenty of power to help your tablet charge completely. Other cables may not be strong enough to deliver enough power to your device. If you find that nothing is working, then you should contact Amazon and have your device replaced.

Computer Doesn't Recognize Device

Some people have found that when they attempt to connect their device to their PC, it does not connect properly. Often, they find the PC won't discover the device, despite it being plugged in. If this is happening for you, here are some solutions you can try:

- Restart your tablet and computer to ensure there are no glitches in either system preventing the device from being found by your computer.
- Fully charge your tablet prior to attempting to plug it into the computer

to ensure there is enough charge for it to be discovered.

- Use a different USB cable, or make sure that you are using the one that came with the device.

If nothing works, you can try a workaround solution, such as using the Amazon Cloud Drive to upload files from your device and then access them from your computer, or from your computer to your Cloud Drive to be accessed by your tablet.

Device Keeps Turning Off

Some Kindle Fire HD tablets have a tendency to turn off randomly, and often on a consistent basis. If you find this is happening to you, there are a few solutions that you can try. First, you want to make sure your battery is properly charged and that it is not shutting down due to a charging issue. Then, you can reset the device by holding the power button down for 40 seconds to force the tablet to turn off. If this doesn't work, ensure that the device is not overheating. If it is overheating, you may need to have Amazon fix or replace your device. If nothing else is working, try factory resetting your device. Occasionally there may be a bug in an application that causes the device to stop functioning properly, so restoring it to factory settings can eliminate this issue. If it persists, contact Amazon to rectify the problem.

Keyboard Types Erratically

Although this is not common, some Kindle Fire HD owners have reported that they have experienced the keyboard typing on its own. If this happens, the first thing you should try is cleaning off your screen. Ensure you do not clean it with water, but rather use a proper screen cleaner and microfiber cloth to wipe down the screen of any potential debris that may be causing it to sense "touch". Next, you can try resetting the device. If this doesn't work, backup your device and then reset it to factory settings to eliminate any potential bugs or glitches that may exist as a result of an application. If the issue persists, you can contact Amazon.

Blue or Purple Haze Around Edges of Screen

If you receive a device and realize there is either a blue or purple haze around the edges of the screen, there is no known resolution. You must contact Amazon to correct this issue, as they will either fix your device, or replace it. However, Amazon did issue a statement explaining that these color hazes are the result of the LED lights they have chosen to use in their device to ensure the correct colors elsewhere in the screen. Still, if you notice that it is particularly bad or that it is affecting your ability to use or enjoy the device, you can contact Amazon to have the issue rectified.

Fire HD Overheating

Some Kindle Fire HD users have noticed that their device tends to overheat on a regular basis. A device warming up as a result of being used is fairly common, but one that overheats is not. If this is happening on an extreme level, it may even cause your device to shut itself down to prevent permanent damage or fire. If this happens, first you want to check what case you have on your device. Some cases do not allow devices to breathe, so having a case on may be causing the issue. Alternatively, you may have installed an app that is causing the device to overheat. Check any applications you installed yourself and consider deleting them one by one to see if this rectifies the issue. If it is still happening, the best thing you can do is contact Amazon for a replacement device.

Email not Updating or Working

This has a tendency to be more of an annoyance than a true problem, but if you find that your email is not working, there are a few things you can do to get around the problem. First, you can try downloading a third-party mail application like Kaiten Mail. Log in as usual and you should begin receiving your email and updates easily. If it still isn't working, Amazon provides a handful of advice on their FAQ page that may be able to help you get your problem solved. Some of these tips include:

- Ensuring that you are connected to Wi-Fi.
- Ensuring that your email account information is accurate and up to date.
- Ensuring that you have chosen the proper email server settings.
- If nothing else works, try completely erasing all data from the application and then logging in once again. (You can do this by going into your settings, choosing the "application" option, tapping "installed applications", choosing "all applications" on the drop-down menu, choosing "email", and then clicking "clear data").
- Lastly, you can restart the device.

No Sound

Begin by ensuring the volume is turned up on your device. If this isn't working, try plugging in headphones and see if you can get the audio working through headphones. If this doesn't work, try doing a hard reset on your device by holding the power button down for 40 seconds. If you are using a case and the problem is with your headphones, try removing the case and plugging in the headphones once again, as sometimes cases can prevent the jack from plugging in all the way. If you are still not getting any audio from your device, you may need to contact Amazon to have the issue rectified.

Stuck on Logo

If your device gets stuck on the logo when starting up, the best thing you can do is try a hard reset. To do this, hold the button down for 40 seconds. This will cause the tablet to shut off. Then, you can simply turn it back on. If this doesn't help, try turning the device off, plugging it in, and then turning it back on. If you are still not getting past the logo sign, try plugging the device into your PC. If the computer does not recognize the device, or you still cannot get it past this point, it may not be working properly on an internal level, meaning it will need to be replaced by Amazon.

Apps Crashing or Not Loading

Many people have experienced applications that either crash or don't completely load on the Kindle Fire HD 8 and 10 tablets. The best thing you can do is try and discover which application it is happening to. Often, it won't happen to all applications, only one. Once you know which application is affecting the device, go into your settings and locate the "Apps and Games" setting. There, you can select "Manage All Applications". Locate the application that is not working on the list, and then choose the "Force Stop" and "Clear Cache" options to force it to quit and erase anything that has been cached within the app. This should eliminate anything that may be causing it not to work properly. It is similar to doing a hard reset on the application. If this still isn't working, try uninstalling the app and then reinstalling it. If it is an external app, meaning it was not originally uploaded when you purchased the device, it may be one that does not work on the device you have.

Not Reading MicroSD Card

If your device is not reading the MicroSD card you have plugged in to your device, start by ensuring the device is fully charged. You may need to plug it in while connecting the SD card as well. Next, you can ensure that all recent updates have been completed on the device. Sometimes a device that has not been updated will not recognize external devices and storage systems correctly. If you have a case on your tablet, you may try removing that as well. Certain cases will prevent the MicroSD card from plugging in properly, preventing it from being recognized by the device. Alternatively, the card may not be configured to work on the device you are using it with. If this is the case, you would want to reset the MicroSD card on your computer first, before plugging it into your device. Note that this will result in all of the files on the card being lost, so back them up to an alternate storage source first before clearing the card.

"An Internal Error Occurred" Message

A variety of Kindle Fire HD tablet users have reported a message showing up on their device preventing them from completing certain functions. The message seems to be erratic, and comes up saying "an internal error occurred". If you receive this message on your device, there are a few steps you can take in order to resolve this issue:

1. Restart your internet router
2. Restart your tablet
3. Force Stop the application that will not load by locating it in the applications section of your settings

4. Ensure the date and time are correct on the device (sometimes this can cause glitches). To do this, enter your device settings and select the "date and time" option, then enter the appropriate information.

5. Deregister the device and register it again. To do this, access the settings on your device, then go to "Account". From there you can "Deregister" your device.

Freezing or Won't Start Up

If the device is freezing or not completely starting up, try restarting the device. Hold the power button down for 40 seconds to force it to restart completely. If this isn't working, try shutting off the device, plugging it in, and then restarting it. Alternatively, plug it in with the device turned off and allow it to charge for a while before attempting to restart it. In this case, the battery may be completely dead or extremely low on power, causing it to struggle to turn on. If it still isn't working, you may need to contact Amazon to consider a replacement device.

Screen Flickering

A screen flicker is common on the Kindle Fire HD 8 and 10, but it can be extremely annoying when you are trying to use the device. If you are experiencing this, you will want to try and rectify the issue. There are two steps you can try to work around this, and a few solutions you can try as well. They are as follows:

1. To try and work around the problem, adjust your brightness. You can find this in the quick settings by swiping down

from the top of the screen. Turning auto-brightness off tends to help with eliminating the screen flicker, although you will have to manually adjust the brightness depending on how bright the room is that you are in.

2. Lock the screen and then unlock it, as this can sometimes help temporarily resolve the problem.

3. Remove a case that may be covering the camera or somehow interrupting the auto-brightness setting. Some cases can cast shadows over the camera, causing it to get confused on what brightness setting to choose.

4. Contact Amazon to resolve the issue, often by replacing the device.

Browser Not Starting or Crashing

The Silk browser is a pre-installed web browsing application that you can use when you turn your device on for the first time. However, it has a tendency to crash or not start. If this is happening for you, you can try a variety of things to overcome this problem. For example, rebooting the device can often help this.

If this is not working, try clearing the data in the browser application. You can do this by going into the settings on your device, choosing the "Manage All Applications" option, and then going into the "All Applications" section. From there, you can choose the Silk Browser application. Once the description screen comes up you can choose "Clear data". This should erase any data that may be causing the browser to malfunction.

If the browser still won't work, try checking your parental control settings. If you have set them, you may have accidentally turned them "on" to control the browser. This would stop anyone from accessing the browser until the settings were adjusted. If you are still having troubles with the Silk browser, try installing and using a different browser application. Some great ones include Maxthon Mobile and Dolphin Browser. These can be downloaded from the application store and have been known to work significantly better than the Silk Browser application.

Other Issue

If you discover any additional troubles on your device, you can try using the built-in help section on the device itself. Amazon built in a section on the settings of the device that allow you to get help if the device is not functioning properly. Simply go into your settings, select "Help & Feedback" and explore the many options available to you. In this section you will find help with many common problems, and this section is updated regularly when your device updates. You can also submit feedback directly to Amazon and get help from the team at Amazon to rectify any further problems you may be having with your device.

Chapter 4: Getting the Most of Kindle Fire

This device isn't only good for basic features! The Kindle Fire tablets were designed to be great customizable devices for anyone who is a fan of the Kindle and Amazon experience. So, if you want to get the maximum use from your device and enjoy it in as many ways as possible, be sure to browse this chapter. From helping you customize your homepage through customizing your favorites to helping you access all of the features on your keyboard and even helping you choose which Bluetooth speaker to use with your device, this chapter will provide you with everything you need to know.

Customizing Your Favorites

At the bottom of your device you can find your "favorites" bar. Here, you can customize your device by adding or changing the applications that are featured. To do this, simply tap and hold the application you want to add or remove from this bar. So, if you want to add one, you would go to the applications menu and drag an application down to the bar. Or, if you want to remove one, you could tap and hold it until a pop-up menu appears, asking if you want to "Remove from Favorites". Select this option and the application will disappear from your favorites menu, but not from your device. If you want to delete it completely, tap "Remove from Device" instead.

General Typing and Text-Entry Tips

Believe it or not, the Kindle Fire HD tablets were installed with cool settings you can use to customize your keyboard. First, you can change the language by holding the space button down. A list of languages will pop up, allowing you to select what language you want your keyboard to display in.

From that same screen, you can tap "Keyboard Settings" and access a variety of settings that you can change on your keyboard. For example, you can choose whether or not the keyboard will make sound when you use it, auto-correct your typing, or complete next-word prediction for you. Other settings you can play with include a personal dictionary of words you use on a regular basis (to prevent them from being auto-corrected), auto-capitalization, and trace typing.

Using Swype Keyboard Feature

Trace typing, which you learned about in the end of the last tip, is also what is known as the Amazon "Swype" keyboard feature. This is a feature where you do not have to tap to type, but rather you can simply swipe your finger across the keyboard, landing on the letters in the word you are wanting to type out. Once you have finished the word, lift your finger for a moment before continuing to type the next word. The brief pause will put a space into your sentence.

Hooking Up to Stereo Speakers

You can connect your Kindle Fire HD to stereo speakers by using the Bluetooth option on your device. To do this, swipe down from the top of the screen to access your quick settings. There, ensure that you have turned on your Bluetooth. Then, turn on the Bluetooth speaker that you intend to use. Use the Bluetooth pairing instructions outlined in Chapter 1 "Bluetooth Pairing". This should connect your device to a Bluetooth speaker so that you can begin listening through larger audio speakers. Note that your device can only play through one speaker at a time, so be sure to choose the correct speaker. Otherwise, you can disconnect your Bluetooth by turning Bluetooth "off" and then turning it back "on" so that you can retry the pairing settings.

External Speaker Options

There are a variety of Bluetooth speakers you can purchase to begin using your Kindle Fire HD Bluetooth speaker option. Some of the most popular varieties include:

- Bose SoundLink Revolve+ (best overall)
- UE Boom 2 (best waterproof speaker)
- B&O Beoplay P2 (best portable speaker)
- DOSS SoundBox Touch (best affordable speaker)

- Bowers & Wilkins Zeppelin Wireless (best high-end speaker)
- Amazon Echo (best smart speaker)

Even if you purchase something that is not listed here, however, as long as it features Bluetooth capabilities you will be able to use it on your device. You can also use Bluetooth headphones, or headphones that connect by a traditional AUX cord.

Skype and Skype Camera

To use Skype and access the camera through Skype on your Kindle Fire HD 8 or 10, simply download the Skype application from your application store. Then, launch the application. Upon launch you will be asked to input your login information. If you do not already have an account with Skype, you will need to create one. Then, you can login. From there, you will see the option to place video calls to other Skype users. These calls are made over Wi-Fi, so they are easy to use on your tablet. Simply "video call" a person and the camera will turn on. You may be prompted to "allow access to the camera" before placing your first call. If so, simply press "allow" and the camera will be able to be used by the Skype application, enabling you to make video calls through Skype.

Basic Security

There are four basic actions you need to take when it comes to protecting your Kindle Fire HD tablet from potential security threats. These security measures are easy, cost nothing, and will protect your device from being used by unauthorized users.

1. Always use the "lock" function on your tablet. Lock your tablet any time you are done using it. Locking it will ensure that anyone without your password will not be able to access your device. If you are unsure about how to set a lock password for your device, follow these steps:

>   Access settings, tap security, and then choose the "Lock Screen" option. There, you can choose to "Turn On Lock Screen Password". The device will prompt you to input your chosen password two times to ensure that you have entered the one you intended to enter. After that, you can confirm the password. Now, anytime you

lock your device, this password will be required to unlock it.

2. Lock down Wi-Fi access. You can do this by going into your settings, tapping "restrictions" and then turning on "enable restrictions". There, you can access a password to protect your Wi-Fi on your device. Then, in order to connect to ANY Wi-Fi networks, that password will be required.

3. Restrict Applications. Kindle Fire HD tablets will naturally restrict apps that are being downloaded from anywhere other than the Amazon App Store itself. If there is any chance this setting has been changed, however, you will want

to ensure that it is set to restrict applications.

4. Clean your browser. The Amazon Kindle Fire HD has a built-in browser application called "Silk". While in it, you can tap the menu icon located at the bottom of the browser's display. There, you will discover the "Settings" for the browser. Tap this and then choose options such as "Clear cookie data, clear cache, and clear browser history". This can prevent your device from being hacked by external sources through your browser.

Parental Controls

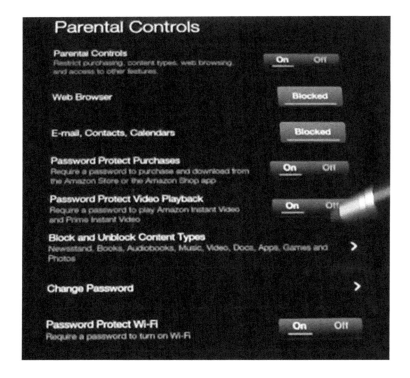

Kindle Fire HD tablets are designed to be family-friendly. For that reason, there are parental controls you can access to help you keep your family safe when using the device. The parental controls can help with everything from restricting browser usage to setting daily time limits on how long your children can use the device for. You can access the Parental Control functions by entering the settings on your device. In case you have forgotten, you can access the settings by swiping down from the top of the screen. Then, select the "more" option. From there, you can select "Parental Controls". Then, you can tap the switch next to this setting to ensure that they are turned "on". From there, you need to enter a password that you wish to use to protect the parental controls from being tampered with by anyone. Once you have chosen your password, confirm it and then tap "finish". From there, you will be able to restrict the following:

- App Store
- Email, Contact and Calendar apps
- Web Browsing
- Camera

- Social Network Sharing Options
- Specific Content (e.g. books, applications, videos, etc.)

In addition to restricting them, you can password protect things such as purchases, Wi-Fi connectivity, playing content through Amazon Video, and location services.

If your controls have been successfully added, a lock will appear in the top corner of the screen. This will disappear if you turn off the parental controls.

Educational Potential

Amazon Kindle Fire HD 8 and 10 tablets have a major educational potential when it comes to using them with children. Many have been implemented into classroom activities as a result of their educational potential. To take advantage of this potential yourself, you can download apps such as "Piqosity". These applications are known for their ability to help children learn. They can help with such things as:

- Classwork (e.g. using the tablets to complete personalized practice problems)
- Homework (e.g. assigning custom practice problems to be completed as homework)
- Monitoring (e.g. allowing teacher to immediately see if homework has been completed or not)
- Analysis (e.g. grading student's work and analyzing their improvements, or not, based on previous results)

In addition to Piqosity, there are other applications such as those that help with learning shapes and colors, learning the alphabet and spelling, learning to read, learning to write, learning to draw, and more. Simply browse the app store for "Educational Apps" to discover a variety of applications that are age-appropriate for a variety of age groups, from children through to adult.

Flashcards and Other Drills

In addition to downloading applications that can help with teaching new things, you can also download applications that help with learning through use of flashcards and other memory-building and skill-building systems. Applications such as "Sight Words Kids Reading Games & Flash Cards" are great for using flash cards directly on the Kindle Fire HD 8 and 10 to teach children all different types of information and educational content. You can even locate customizable applications that can allow you to generate the content of your choosing on each flashcard.

Productivity Potential

The Kindle Fire HD 8 and 10 tablets have a variety of applications and games dedicated directly to productivity. These can help with everything from note taking to remembering stuff, and even transferring content to other people or devices. Applications such as "OneNote", "Dropbox", "Evernote" and "PDF Max" can all help when it comes to increasing productivity with the applications.

In some work places, bosses have provided a variety of people on the floor with tablets that can be used to link all workers together. This can make note taking, scheduling, and even sharing presentations and other important documents significantly easier.

Conclusion

Thank you for reading *"New Kindle Fire HD Manual (Kindle Fire HD 8 and 10): The complete user guide with instructions from basic start up to advance user (December 2017)"*.

This user guide was designed to help you begin using, continue using, and getting the most out of your device. If you were experiencing any issues with your device, this guide also has a variety of information to help you get the most out of your device.

I hope that you were able to learn everything that you were interested in learning when it comes to using your Kindle Fire HD tablet. If you were wanting to learn more about basic functions, how to access hidden features such as your camera, or how to troubleshoot common issues, then I hope you were able to find that information within this guidebook.

The next step is to keep this book handy on your tablet so that you can access it anytime you are in need of help with your device. Whether you need to recall how to access certain functions, or if you are interested in learning how you can make the most out of your device, you can access everything you need in this one easy book. To get to the book on your device, ensure you download it on your Kindle Fire tablet and simply access the "book" section of your device to get instant access to this book on your tablet.

Lastly, if you enjoyed this book and felt that it helped you with your Kindle Fire HD experience, I ask that you please rate it on Amazon. Your honest feedback would be greatly appreciated. (To do so, return to the product detail of this very guidebook and click "Write a customer review". There, you can fill out your review and "Submit" it so I can see how much you enjoyed this book! Thank you!)

Thank you!

Check Out Other Books

Please go here to check out other books that might interest you:

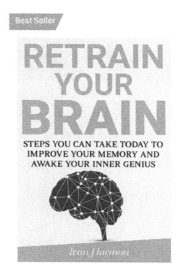

Retrain Your Brain: Steps You Can Take Today to Improve Your Memory and Awake Your Inner Genius by Ivan Harmon

Enhance Memory: Find Out How Memory

Functions, Switch On Your Brain and Have

Better Memory - two-book bundle

by Ivan Harmon

Boost Your Brain Power: Learn Better, Smarter, and faster - Scientifically Proven Guides to Sharpen Your Focus and Retrain Your Brain by Ivan Harmon

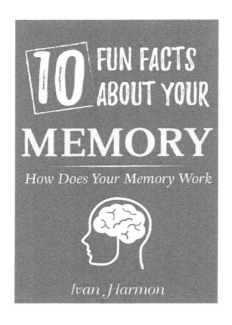

10 Fun Facts About Your Memory

by Ivan Harmon

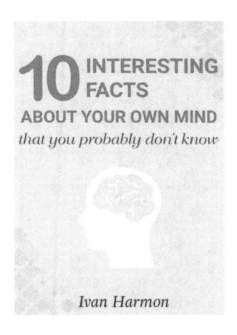

10 Interesting Facts About Your Own Mind that

You Probably Don't Know

by Ivan Harmon

Switch On Your Brain: 10 Fun and Interesting Facts About Your Own Mind that You Want to Know by Ivan Harmon

Memory Exercises: Create a habit for memory enhancement by Ivan Harmon

Have Better Memory: Your Memory How It

Works and How to Improve It by Ivan Harmon

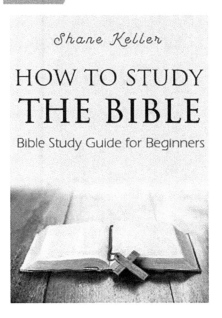

How to Study the Bible: Bible Study Guide for

Beginners by Shane Keller

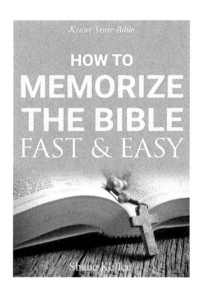

Know your Bible: How to Memorize the Bible
Fast and Easy
by Shane Keller

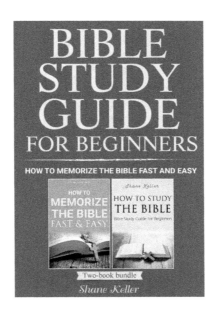

Bible Study Guide for Beginners: How to
Memorize the Bible Fast and Easy
by Shane Keller

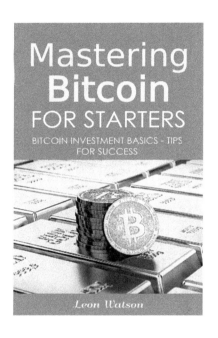

Mastering Bitcoin for Starters: Bitcoin

Investment Basics - Tips for Success

by Leon Watson

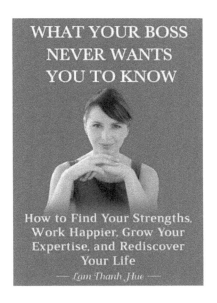

What Your Boss Never Wants You to Know:

How to Find Your Strengths, Work Happier,

Grow Your Expertise, and Rediscover Your Life

by Lam Thanh Hue

www.ingramcontent.com/pod-product-compliance
Lightning Source LLC
LaVergne TN
LVHW052305060326
832902LV00021B/3711